Zen
in the Blink of an Eye

Scott Shaw

Buddha Rose Publications

Zen in the Blink of an Eye
Copyright 2007 by Scott Shaw
www.scottshaw.com
ALL RIGHTS RESERVED

First Edition 2007

Library of Congress Control Number:
2009938270

ISBN: 1-877792-41-1
ISBN-13: 978-1877792410

No part of this book may be reproduced in any manner without the expressed written permission of the author or the publishing company.

10 9 8 7 6 5 4 3 2 1

Printed in the United States of America

Zen
in the Blink of an Eye

One

Zen equals simplicity.

Many people want Zen to equal

>Practices,
>Techniques,
>Discipline,
>Religion,
>and the promise of Nirvana someday.

They miss the point.

Two

Life is a pathway of continuations.

The first is set in motion for us;
    our pathway from Birth to Death.

Other pathways are dominated by our physical, social, and economic environment.

Within the constraints of these predetermined pathways we forge out our own destiny.

Then, like a river carving its way through a canyon as it flows to the sea, we dig ourselves in deeper and deeper.

    Breakdown the boundaries of your walls.
    Interrupt the trail of known-ness.
    Experience the expansive emptiness.

    This is Zen.

Three

Zen is an abstract science.

Abstract because it leads the practitioner down a road to embrace the understanding of

No-Definition.

A science because it has an end result,

Enlightenment.

Four

When we see an object for the first time we search our minds for a determination of what it is.

When we find a suitable answer,
                    a definition is set in place.

Definitions limit reality.

If you let go of the knowing,
    everything is allowed to exist within its own essence.

Existing within its own essence,
    everything becomes a perfect reflection of itself.

Five

Religion is like Algebra,
    A + B = C.
But, Algebra only works
    if you know what A and B are.

Zen is like poetry.
    It doesn't have to make any sense.
    It just is.

Six

In the physical world

> *This is This*
> and
> *That is That.*

All is bound by duality.

In Zen,

This and That have no meaning because everything is merged into oneness.

Seven

Believing you know the answer to the question keeps you from the truth.

The Zen mind is the no-mind.
Knowing nothing you are allowed to simply *Be*.

This is where Nirvana is found.

Eight

Many people believe that they must run away and hide from the physical world if they ever hope to obtain spiritual understanding.

        Retreating serves a purpose.
            But, escape is only escape.

You can never escape from yourself.

        This is the paradoxical gift of life,

            you have a body,
            you have a mind,

        and you can choose move beyond
        the limitations of your body and your mind.

Nine

The path to Self-Realization is very obvious.

It is simply confused by

>thoughts,
>ideas,
>desires,
>knowledge,
>and religion.

Ten

People love to tell you how it is.

People love to speak about what they know to be true.

>People can talk,
>but talk is not the truth.
>
>Talk is only talk.
>
>The true knower says nothing.
>
>With this, the pure essence is all that remains.

Eleven

Nirvana knows no seeking.

Nirvana comes when seeking has stopped.

Twelve

Meditation is not difficult.

The reason people believe meditation is difficult is because they fight the naturalness of it.

Thirteen

Zazen means, *"To sit in Zen."*

Teachers for centuries have laid down techniques for meditation:

>Sit, legs locked,
>eyes fixed three feet in front of you.
>
>With each in-breath
>count, *"One."*
>
>With each out-breath
>count, *"Two."*
>
>Is Zazen defined by technique?
>
>No.
>   *Technique is only technique.*

To sit in Zen occurs when you forgo technique and simply become.

Fourteen

Transition.

By moving from one life activity immediately onto the next you lose the essence of each part of life and all of your existence becomes a non-stop blur.

    Step away from one space with presence.

    Step into new space with presence.

    Know each.

    Define the subtitles.

    Then, life is known as life,
    meditation is experienced as meditation,
    and all becomes a never ending process of continual realization.

Fifteen

Life equals doing.

You can do things because you have to do them.

You can love or you can hate the process every step of the way.

Or, you can make your *DOING* art.

    Beauty is in the eye of the beholder.

Sixteen

If you surround yourself by what is known, you never allow yourself to experience anything new.

Seventeen

Many people live their lives in Auto-mode.
They pass though their physical existence with out a
though -- doing what they are suppose to do.

> *Doing equals Doing,*
> *until Doing can be done no more.*
>
> *Un-Doing equals Buddha-Mind,*
> where you free yourself from the known and
> expected and exist in pure essence.
>
> > *Do or Undo,*
> > two paths,
> > two results.

Eighteen

If you choose to have a preference
you may not like what you are experiencing.

If you let go of the way you want things to be
Every-Thing exists within its own perfection.

Nineteen

Everyday there are millions of

    sights,
    sounds,
    and experiences to witness.

You can look out and be guided by them.
Or, you can look in and not be controlled.

Twenty

Life is life.
We must walk the path we walk.

> Because life is life,
> the holy move among us.
> We may not even notice them
> because they say nothing
> and do nothing to draw attention to
> themselves.
>
> *Holiness is not loud or obvious.*

Twenty-one

You can think you know.
That is belief.

You can tell others you know.
That is teaching.

You can let go of knowing
and embrace the truth.

      That is Zen.

Twenty-two

It is the doorway
>that allows you to enter a building.

Once inside,
>you are enclosed by walls.

It is your thought of *I-ness* that holds you locked into your separation from cosmic realty.

Walk outside and embrace the wholeness.

Twenty-three

You can look to the heavens for answers.
You can question, *"Why?"*

You can blame and seek restitution.
Or, you can let go, accept each event as an expression of the perfection of life, and understand that right or wrong is only defined by your perceptions.

> From this, you will be free.
> You will not need to question, *"Why?"*

One path holds you to the ways of the world.

Once path guides you down the road to Nirvana.

> *Your life.*
> *Your choice.*

Twenty-four

If you place money in front of you,
you will think about money.

If you place an image of the Buddha in front of you,
you will think about the Buddha.

What do you want to think about?

Twenty-five

I can be me.
You can be you.
We can be in a place together
and never understand anything about one another.

Why?
Because the individual mind locks itself into its own
self-worth.

    More or less,
    better or worse,
    higher and lower
    are not Zen.
        That is mind.

    No higher and no lower,
    no near and no far,
    no right and no wrong,
        that is Nirvana.

Twenty-six

The fast paced,
      highly structured world teaches us to be:

            rushed,
            confrontational,
            desirous,
            envious,
            and angry.

Twenty-seven

Zen teaches you to sit in the midst of chaos and be at peace.

Twenty-eight

What do you know?

Where did that knowledge come from?

Why do you believe your knowledge to be real?

> You can believe
> > or you can become.
>
> Believing keeps you locked into definition.
> > Definitions always change.
>
> Becoming lets you flow into
> > Cosmic Consciousness,
>
> > > moving with each change like
> > > the waves upon the ocean.

Twenty-nine

The truth speaks to you from everywhere.

>Open your eyes,
>open your mind,
>and your path will become clear.

Thirty

You can hate what you are doing.
Or, you can love what you are doing.

Hate causes strain in the
       space-time-realization-continuum.

Love allows you to be calm even in the face of adversity.

How do you come to love what you hate?
Let go of your predetermined definitions of how you believe something should feel.

By letting go,
you allow every action and ever reaction to exist within its own perfection.

Existing within its own perfection,
each action transcends its physical limitations and moves towards the greater good.

Thirty-one

Many people believe that physical objects make them holy.
Many people believe that divine symbols and images will protect them.

    Holy?
        What is that?
    Protection?
        From what?

    Let go and be.
    Embraces totality.

Then, holiness becomes an abstract point of view.

And safety?

    Who can hurt the wind?

Thirty-two

We construct our pathways to heaven.
Higher and higher, we try to touch the divine.

    But, divinity is right here, right now.

    Look no further but in this place.

        In this moment,
                right where you find yourself.

Thirty-three

In 1271 Marco Polo left Venice, Italy on his journey to Asia. After two decades he returned home.

How many people have traveled to Asia to find the truth?

How many people have come home simply to forgo their ideology and re-embrace a life lived among the mainstream?

Does a place give you the truth?

Thirty-four

Siddhartha Guatama, the Sakyamuni Buddha,
walked among us as a man.

When his physical body was no longer with us
people made him a divine entity worthy of worship.

You can worship the Buddha
but worship is only worship.
Worship is not enlightenment.

As long as you worship,
you can not become one with the Buddha-Mind.

Let go of worship and understand the essential
teaching of Zen,

>*"We all are enlightened."*

Thirty-five

Zen is about *No-Thing-Ness*.

Yet, so many people claim that what they know is right and what another knows is wrong.

> *If what is, is,*
> *how can there be a right or a wrong?*

Thirty-six

There is an image of yourself that you wish to project to the world.

And then there is what is.

You can hide.
You can conceal your *outside-ness*.
But, the internal truth never changes.

Thirty-seven

Sanga
It has long been taught that one should congregate with those of similar mind.

Where do you find your Sanga?

Thirty-eight

So much of our lives are defined by a belief of who we are, as we are doing what we believe we are supposed to do.

    Step outside of your framework,

              and who do you become?

Thirty-nine

We build structures for worship.

        But, structures do not last.

This exemplifies the temporary-ness of our beliefs.

        Structure without structure,

                the essence of Zen.

Forty

Passion is invigorating.

    Religion is passion.
        Passion for a belief.

People love because of passion.
People lust because of passion.
People feel alive because of passion.
People die because of passion.

But, People are not enlightened
because of passion.

    Only stimulated.

Forty-one

You can look outside
and witness the beauty.

You can look inside
and focus upon all of your faults.

Or, you can realize that the idealized image of how you expect holiness to appear and why you are not worthy of it is only your own internal projection which ultimately keeps you from realizing that you possess all of the necessary elements for Self-Realization.

>What are the necessary elements
>for Self-Realization?

>Life.

Forty-two

For centuries people have sought Nirvana
believing that it is the ultimate goal of human existence.

    Nirvana is not a goal.
    Nirvana is absent from achievement.

    By making Nirvana a goal,
    you separate yourself from Nirvana.

    Nirvana is,
    when you are not.

Forty-three

We seek calm.
      We seek peace.
           We look for it outside of ourselves.

You can run from noise.
You can hide from confusion.
You can attempt to place yourself in an environment where it cannot find you.

But, like the waves of the ocean,
one minute calm,
the next crashing against the shore,
you can not control nature
or the creations of humanity.

You can, however, learn to control how you experience and react to them.

      Become silent within yourself.

Forty-four

When you enter a sanctuary full of mind,
knowing what you know,
followed by a trail of past deeds,
the sanctuary becomes saturated with your Karma
and there is no peace to be found.

Enter a sanctuary free of mind,
then the essence of cosmic suchness is allowed to permeate you.

Forty-five

You can be guided by a teacher.

But, it is you who must come to touch the essence of the teachings if you wish to understand the absolute truth of the universe.

Forty-six

Stop,
close your eyes,
breath.

Listen,
experience all that is around you.

Let your mind travel through your body.
Mentally encounter each element of your physical form:
> your toes,
> your feet,
> your legs,
> your fingers,
> your arms,
> your torso,
> your neck,
> your head.

Now, realize that you are not these external elements.

You simply are the essence that inhabits your physical being.

> *Form of the formless,*
> *the key to Zen.*

Forty-seven

When we step back and view the essence of what we consume,

                is the acquisition worth the cost?

Forty-eight

If your sights are set somewhere far off in the distance, you cannot see the beauty of what is in front of you.

In Zen, the going is the coming.

You are already there.

Forty-nine

If you desire to desire.

Desire is like the roar of the mighty dragon.
It is all encompassing.

How much of your *Life-Time* have you spend thinking of what you wished you possessed?

How many times have you desired something,

>then once you obtained it,
>you desired it no more?

>Desires lasts only as long as the desire lasts.

>Desire is an addiction.
>Desire will hold you confined
>by the on-going
>turmoil of the material world.

>>Do you want desire?
>>Or, do you want to touch Satori?

>Like all things in life,
>it is your choice.

Fifty

More or less is a perspective.

People wish to help those they believe to be less than themselves.

You cannot help the lesser,
      unless you see yourself as more.

As long as you believe that you are more and have something to give another person,
              you are bound by maya.

Believing in the falsehood of more or less, you are not embracing the ultimate perfection of all living and non-living entities.

      See what you see,
      that is life.
      Embracing the essential totality,
      that is Zen.

Fifty-one

Illumination comes when you forgo the restraints of what is known, even if only for a moment.

In that moment, the hidden light of the Eternal Mind is revealed.

Once revealed, it is never forgotten.

Fifty-two

People attempt to make non-believers believe.
People attempt to make the non-spiritual spiritual.
People judge those who are not on the path to realization or in the same spiritual tradition as somehow less.

> *Less is more.*
> *The untruth is the ultimate truth.*
> *The non-spiritual are, in fact, the truly spiritual because they do not judge those who are not on the spiritual path.*

Judgment, at any level, is not Zen.

Fifty-three

At the heart of Zen is understanding.

Understanding is based in letting all things be as they are.

Fifty-four

You can crusade for what you believe in.
You can fight for what you know to be right.
But, right or wrong is based solely upon your own personal judgment.

How many people have died in the name of religion?

> *Let go and let all life be.*
> *This is Zen humanity.*

Fifty-five

Step into peace
and peace will be you.

You can walk from one place to another.
You can do whatever it is you want to do.
But, *Doing* keeps you busy.
Busy, you are forever lost in never ending tasks.

    Was the Buddha busy?

        Do without Doing
        and everything is done.

Fifty-six

Zen is not about hiding from your emotions.
That is denial.

Zen is not about repressing your feelings.
That is discipline.

Zen is not about personal gain and power.
That is business.

Zen is about realizing that one desire leads to the next and that you will never embrace spiritual freedom if you do not choose to let your desires go instead of allowing them to control you.

Ultimately, Zen is about choice.

Choosing enlightenment
over desiring the world.

Fifty-seven

Many people wish to become something other than what they are.

> *Becoming* is a pathway.
> A pathway never ends until it ends.

Where one pathway ceases another one begins.

> Why do people want to *Become?*

Because they believe that they are not enough.

Society and religion portray idealized images.

> You must be
> richer,
> prettier,
> better employed,
> holier.

Have you met the richer, prettier, better employed, or the holier?

They walk a pathway seeking greater perfection, as well.

> *Be*
> and there is nothing more to *Become.*

Fifty-eight

Seeking is only seeking.

    It ends within itself.

Fifty-nine

You can create images to worship the Buddha.
You can hide secret teachings within your art.

But, did the Buddha worship himself?

    No.

Did the Buddha ask to be worshiped?

    No.

The Buddha taught that everybody could realize enlightenment.

Realization is not defined by worship or hidden teachings.

Realization is absent from those physical manifestations.

Sixty

If you step beyond the control of what is expected,

if you move into the pure expression of what is,

then you are free and you have nothing more to become.

Sixty-one

If you are looking to other to blame for your current situation
>you are looking in the wrong direction.

>You are the center of your universe.

>Actualize it.

Sixty-two

The clothing you wear
defines who you are.
But clothing can be changed.

A monk can put on a suit.
Does that make him less of a monk?

Let go of the images.
Forget definitions.
Then you see beyond the expected and the known.

This is where realization is born.

Sixty-three

It has been taught for centuries that one must meditate without movement. Sit firm like a rock.

Is a statue the perfect example of meditation?

You can sit and pretend to be a rock.

Or, you can sit and become one with all.

Sixty-four

Empty yourself.

Sixty-five

There is a place in all of us where true peace exists.

>Find it.
>Go there,

>even in the most intense circumstances.

Sixty-six

If you will open your eyes to the subtleties of obviousness, you will find many teachings, guiding you on your Spiritual Path.

Sixty-seven

You can look out.
Or, you can look in.

Looking out promises a world of beauty, ugliness, and desires.

Looking in, promises enlightenment.

Sixty-eight

We construct shrine for the gods we worship.

Sixty-nine

Conscious interaction with all living things is a pathway to the divine.

Seventy

You can build walls to protect yourself.

But, hiding keeps you locked into the prison that you have created.

      No walls.
           No limitations.

Seventy-one

If you let someone engage you in battle,
  you must fight the war.

With nothing to win and nothing to lose,
  there is no reason to fight.

Zen is about the Non-Fight.

Seventy-two

Life is full of intricacies.

Seek the source point.

Let go of the manifestations.

You will encounter the Universal Essence.

Seventy-three

Is a specific place holy?
Or, do we make it holy?

Does holiness emanate from a location?

> Is holiness only experienced by the individual who has the mind to perceive its presence?
>
> Or, is holiness universal?

Seventy-four

The essence of purity and divinity
   is all around you.

   Look and you will see.

Seventy-five

We pray for what we want.
If we get it,
      we pray for something more.

      Praying is not the pathway to Nirvana.
      Praying is the pathway to desire.

Seventy-six

Life is like a flame in the wind.

The flame needs oxygen to exist,
        but a sudden gust of air will blow it out.

Embrace the *temporary-ness* of your existence.

Seventy-seven

Before enlightenment, *chop wood, carry water.*
After enlightenment, *chop wood, carry water.*

Think about it.

Life is based on *Doing.*

The secret to Zen:

Inaction within action.

Seventy-eight

From history we can learn.

But, history is not an element of your current moment.

>   History is gone.
>   You are now.

>   You can hold onto the past,
>   look to it for answers
>   but the answers found in the past are not
>   your realizations,
>   they are truths experienced by another
>   person in another time.

>   Live your moment.
>   Come to know your own truths.

Seventy-nine

Construction and Destruction,
    the two primary patterns of life.

The world teaches us to create.

We are told that this is the way to fulfillment.

Construction is not organic.
    It requires external objects and other people to achieve creation.

    To create,
    we alter nature.
    Reshape it and reform it into new patterns.

        Creation destroys other forms of life.
        So, Construction is Destruction.

    Is this the way of Zen?

    Zen is the pathway of Un-Creation.

Eighty

Zen is like insanity.

It has you step outside of the known
        and the accepted.

Eighty-one

Stop right now.

      Right where you are.

Embrace divine knowledge.

Eighty-two

You can tell the world who you are
    or you can *Be*.

        Being is.
        Telling is not.

Eighty-three

Why do teachers teach
>that you must be disciplined?

>That you must sit for hours in meditation
>to ever find Nirvana?

>Because they have not experienced it.

They have been told a story which has been repeated a million different times, in a thousand different languages.

Enlightenment does not take discipline.

Discipline is for the worldly individual.

>Enlightenment comes naturally.

>Let go of desire.
>Let go of wanting Nirvana.
>Experience the wholeness naturally.
>And, Nirvana will come to you.

Eighty-four

Look for the hidden object shrouded deeply within the image.

When you find it, you will win a prize.

How many spiritual traditions have propagated a teaching which promises enlightenment only if you can find a secret mystery concealed deeply within the discipline?

If someone tells you the truth is hidden or is unobtainable, they do not know the truth.

Enlightenment is right here, right now.

Be it and you will know it.

Eighty-five

In any moment
        you can step into the perfection.

        How?
        Let go
        and embrace the entireness.

Eighty-six

Most people believe that they are not enlightened.

In Zen it is understood that we all are enlightened. Most simply do not wish to embrace this absolute truth.

It is easier to feel unworthy,

>know that you are not pure enough,
>know that you have not
>practiced long enough.
>
>Practice is addiction.
>It is *Doing* instead of *Becoming*.
>
>In the *Doing* there is purpose.
>In the *Becoming* all need for purpose is lost.

The way to the enlightenment is easy.

>*Let go and know.*

Eighty-seven

In the end,
> nature always overcomes the temporary-ness
> of human life.

Creations fall,
> and all returns to a natural balance.

Eighty-eight

You can think about things
  all day long if you want to.

You can judge and criticize everything,
  if that is what makes you feel fulfilled.

You can do whatever you want.

But, you will never know unless you let go.

Eighty-nine

There are always new mountains to climb if you look to the horizon.

If you look inside, you realize that the outside has nothing to offer, as it is all so temporary.

Ninety

Thinking chains you to the way you believe things to be.

True knowing is beyond thought.

Ninety-one

If you want it
        you can find a way to get it.

      Not wanting is liberation.

Ninety-two

Life is full of noise.
There is movement all around us.

    We can move
           or we can be still.

    Stillness in the movement,
        this is Zen.

Ninety-three

The Buddha was not a Buddhist.
He wandered Hindu India seeking the truth.

When Buddha obtained realization,
he still was not a Buddhist.
He was an enlightened being.

Enlightened beings do not need to worship the gods. Why worship when you have become interactive with the Divine Essence?

Ninety-four

If you are picturing your future,
> you are not living your now.

No Now/No Future.

When it gets here,
> you will simply be picturing something else.

Ninety-five

Hidden in the most unlikely environments
is the simplicity of the truth.

> Without predetermined definition,
> you allow yourself to experience it.

Ninety-six

If you ask an enlightened person to tell you something spiritual,

    they have noting to say.

Ninety-seven

We see an image once
and it is new, unique, and intriguing.

We see it twice
and it is known and expected.

      Expected keeps you from realization.

      See everything for the first time.

Ninety-eight

You can feel what you feel.
That is life.

You can mentally control your pains
and disable your emotions,
that is discipline.

You can consciously
be good to all humanity,
that is kindness.

You can see good
in all that is bad,
that is understanding.

Or, you can step beyond the maya that makes you believe that all of the momentary components that make up this physical world, including your life, are real and eternal,

                that is Zen.

Ninety-nine

The end of one
      creates the beginning of two.

One Hundred

The temple is not external,
    it is in you.

        You can walk out
            or, you can walk in.

Walking out,
    you meet all the glories of human existence:
        emotions,
        happiness,
        sadness,
        love,
        hate,
        desire,
        and accomplishment.

Walking in,
    you encounter your True Spiritual Essence.

One Hundred-one

Life is lived,
        then it is gone.

Objects created
        are objects which will disintegrate.

        Nothing lasts forever.

This is the perfection of existence.

        Eternal cleansing.

The more you fight it,
        the more miserable you become.

The more you accept it,
        the freer you become.

              Live and let go.

One Hundred-two

You love what you love
        until you do not love it anymore.

This is why love is not the pathway to realization.
It is only the pathway to emotion.

      Zen is Emotion-Less

One Hundred-three

The mysteries are hidden
    but they are not hard to see.

One Hundred-four

Cages are created to bind your possessions.

    Possessions hold you bound
    to the ways of the world.

    What cages have you created for yourself?

One Hundred-five

When you embrace the absolute

    the mundane becomes cosmic art.

One Hundred-six

You are alive.
As such, you are a part of every-thing
which take place on this Earth.

>What you think
>and what you do
>sets a million unseen, unknown
>actions and reactions in motion.

Do not believe that just because you are not in the middle of a cataclysmic event, that you have not taken part in it.

>*Life is your Karma.*

One Hundred-seven

Stop looking outside.

    Seek inspiration within yourself.

One Hundred-eight

The thought of no thought.

Knowing without knowing.

The Zen pathway to Cosmic Consciousness.

www.ingramcontent.com/pod-product-compliance
Lightning Source LLC
Chambersburg PA
CBHW072010090426
42734CB00033B/2328